YOUR TOWN

A DESTINATION

The 25 Immutable Rules of Successful Tourism

Destination
Development, Inc.

Roger A. Brooks
& Maury Forman

Copyright ©2003 by Destination Development, Inc.

©2006 Destination Development, Inc. Second edition

Published by:
Destination Development, Inc.
510 Custer Way Suite 301 Olympia, WA 98501
Washington State Department of Community, Trade & Economic Development
PO Box 42525 Olympia, WA 98504-2525

ISBN 978-0-9724855-1-7

Printed in the United States of America
10 9 8 7 6 5 4 3 2 1

Cover photo: Downtown Cambria, California.
Photo this page: Downtown Greenville, South Carolina.

Contents

Acknowledgments

There may be 25 immutable rules for tourism, but there is only one immutable rule in writing a book. It is the rule of thanks. There are a number of people who have helped us with this book by doing research, coming up with ideas, and editing. Writing a book is similar to planning a trip. It is usually a group effort, and this book would never have come together if it had not been for a number of people that made this public-private partnership possible.

We are very grateful for the excellent input and editing by Sandra Prater. Her keen eye for details helped make the book more readable and practical for communities interested in further developing their tourism industry.

We would like to thank Juli Wilkerson, Director of the Washington State Department of Community, Trade and Economic Development (CTED); Larry Williams, Assistant Director for International Trade and Economic Development, CTED; and Linda Alongi, Education and Training Program Manager, CTED, for their support of this project. They provide continued assistance for educational tools such as this book, knowing that education and training are part of a successful economic development program.

The 25 Immutable Rules of Successful Tourism was introduced at the nationally recognized Northwest Economic Development Games in Ellensburg, Washington in 1996, as a two-hour multi-media workshop. Since that time, this presentation has been seen in hundreds of communities throughout North America and often followed by an in-depth and practical community assessment. The team at Destination Development deserves a lot of credit for years of research, finding anecdotal stories and case histories from throughout North America. Thanks especially to Rebecca Durkin and Jane Brooks for their unwavering support, input, and editing in getting both editions of this book published.

We would also like to thank Eric Sheckler for his assistance in procuring photos. And finally, we would like to thank Cheryl Rasch, Washington State Tourism, CTED, for her assistance in securing some excellent photography from the State of Washington's tourism website, which can be viewed at www.experiencewashington.com.

For more information visit:
www.destinationdevelopment.com

Introduction

*W*hat can take months to plan yet is often over in just a few days or weeks? Can be done in a car, train, boat or plane? May cost a whole lot or very little? Requires little (and sometimes nothing) in the way of clothing? Almost always brings people and even nations together? Travel, of course.

Whether for business, pleasure, or rest and relaxation, almost everyone longs to travel. Traveling to Atlanta to synch a business deal might be the trip of a lifetime for a business executive. A family hiking trip through the Sonora Desert might be the beginning of a shared passion for a young family. Or maybe your experience with travel has been more like the Griswold family in National Lampoon's Vacation. Chevy Chase plays the hapless suburbanite from Chicago, traveling with his family across America looking for fun and relaxation. Although everything is planned, nothing goes right. The family endures wrong turns, misleading promotions, rude employees, multiple parking tickets, and unwanted relatives. Yet nothing deters Clark Griswold from spending two memorable weeks with his wife and kids. And apparently, he's not alone.

The family vacation has made a long-awaited comeback, but it looks a bit different. Families are traveling in cars and RVs more often than planes. Some of them are more likely to take several extended-weekend jaunts rather than one annual two-week trip. Many vacationers avoid the hassle of travel by discovering attractions in their own backyards. Entertainment destinations are taking the backseat to trips to discover family heritage or explore the arts. People are less likely to stay with family and friends and more likely to strike out on their own. They are more likely to look for things to do rather than things to see. And, they are spending a lot more money in the process.

Tourism is quickly becoming the "industry of choice" in many communities, while in others it has become "the industry because we have no other choice." Thousands of communities, particularly in rural areas across North America, have seen drastic cutbacks in the industries on which they were founded. Mining, agriculture, fishing, and timber are among the many industries that have seen dramatic cutbacks and closures over the past 20 years. As a result, nearly every community wants to diversify, and tourism seems to be the most natural and easiest diversification strategy.

With thousands of communities considering entering or expanding their tourism industries, we have entered a new age of tourism: the age of specialization. With so many more choices and information instantly at our fingertips, what does your community have that the traveler can't get closer to home? What makes your town worth a special trip?

Tourism As an Economic Development Strategy

Less than a decade ago, cities and towns never considered tourism as an economic development strategy. Yet today, thousands are developing and promoting the industry and see it as a vital part of their economies. The strategy behind tourism is to "import" more cash into your community than you "export." When people earn money in your town and spend some of it elsewhere, it's referred to as "leakage." Communities with a successful tourism industry import more cash than they export and stem the leak.

Tourism has many economic advantages. For example, tourism:

"Leakage" occurs when people who live and work in your community spend some of their money elsewhere. Tourism is the number one method to recapture that loss. Successful tourism happens when your town imports more money from people who visit, spend, and leave than it exports from people who work and live in your town and spend their money elsewhere. Successful communities are subsidized by visitors rather than subsidizing visitors. Which category does your town fall under?

- Diversifies the economy so that communities are no longer dependent on one or two industries.

- Provides a multiplier effect where many businesses, including non-tourism industries, benefit economically.

- Brings in "new money" that creates growth in a community.

- Increases the tax base that helps pay for community amenities and services.

- Creates a variety of business opportunities for entrepreneurs.

- Provides jobs and experience for entry-level workers.

- Promotes business development. Today's visitor might be tomorrow's investor, something which is seen more often in rural areas.

- Boosts appearance and makes the community visually appealing.

Tourism's economic benefit is easily quantified. In the United States alone, tourism:
- Is a $1.3 trillion industry (2006).
- Generates $163 billion in annual wages and salaries.
- Generates $100 billion in local, state and federal taxes.

Tourism is the fastest growing industry (and one of the top three) in all 50 states and in every Canadian province. If economic development is about creating community wealth, then tourism is an important strategy for every community to consider.

What Is A Destination?

There are as many different kinds of visitors as there are people, with as many different reasons for choosing a destination. A destination can be defined as the ending point of any trip. It can be a state park, a festival, the home of relatives or friends, or an attraction.

What Are These "Immutable Rules"?

The Immutable Rules are 25 recommendations your community should implement if you want to make **Your Town a Destination**, drawing visitors and their cash to the area. Travel might be flexible, but the rules to creating a tourist destination are not. The rules you are about to read are immutable because they are absolute and incontrovertible. In other words, they work!

The 25 rules in this book are designed to provide simple ways to make tourism a profitable undertaking by attracting the right kind of visitors and getting them to stay longer. Getting them to stay longer is the ticket, of course, because the longer they stay, the more they spend. After all, overnight visitors spend three times that of day visitors, and infinitely more than pass-through visitors. The more the visitor spends in your community, the less you, the local resident, will have to pay for better streets, law enforcement, and the public amenities you enjoy.

In order to be successful in making your community a destination:
1. You must be able to get passers-by to stop.
2. You need to create ways to keep them in town longer.
3. You should strive for your community to become an overnight or multi-day destination.

Are You Looking for Tourists or Visitors?

If increasing tourism in your community is part of your plans, let's start by defining

"tourist." The traditional meaning of tourist is a person traveling away from home for leisure purposes. The tourism industry usually considers anyone traveling at least fifty miles from home — for any purpose — a tourist. If someone comes into your town from out of town, that person is a "tourist."

We prefer using the word "visitor," because "tourist" implies only the leisure traveler. "Visitors" include business travelers, as well. After all, business travel is a primary source of imported dollars for communities. So, when we refer to "visitors" in this book, we are including people visiting friends and family, business travelers, convention and trade show attendees, passers-by simply stopping for gas and/or food, parents visiting kids in

college, and the occasional visitor who is just there to have a good time.

To the visitor, a vacation is a way to create memories. The Griswold family of National Lampoon fame, and the other Griswold's of the world, remember the time they spent with friends and family, the destinations they visited, the experiences they shared, and the items they bought. The trip really had no rules other than to have fun together. But for the community to benefit more wholly from the Griswold visit, another set of rules would have been required. Here's one: it costs a whole lot less to bring the same visitors back again than it does to keep getting new ones.

Rule I

Can you imagine building your dream home without a set of plans? The result would be a quirky set of misaligned walls and stairs leading nowhere, perhaps suitable as a tourist attraction in its own right, but not that livable.

In fact, that's just what the wealthy heiress, Sarah Winchester, did in San Jose, California. To foil evil spirits, she continually built onto her existing mansion. There are 2,000 doors (that's an average of twelve per room), forty staircases, and numerous secret passages. It is so complex that even the mistress of the manor required a map to get around. And after her death, the Winchester Mystery House did indeed become a popular visitor attraction.

Winchester House is the exception to the rule; most communities do not wish to be known for their lack of planning. Too many communities use the shotgun approach: "Let's run an ad here, let's send a press release there, we need another sign over there...." Without continuity, you cannot build an industry that will stand the test of time.

As a community, you need to bring together your partners to plan what type of tourism activities will bring outside dollars into the area. The outcome of this process will be your

Tourism Development and Marketing Plan, a blueprint that every community should have. It will include strategies for both product development and marketing and encompass every rule in this book. The plan should be so detailed that anyone can follow its recommendations and build a thriving tourism industry.

People can be attracted to your community by any of four different features:
1. Natural resources (lakes, forests, wildlife, recreation)
2. Cultural resources (history, cuisine, ethnic)
3. Human resources (performing arts, craftsmen, artisans)
4. Capital resources (transportation, hotels, utilities)

Understanding the types of resources that are available and how they best fit into the overall plan is critical in getting your community on someone's radar.

After a community identifies what it has that sets it apart from every other community, finding out who to target becomes a little easier. Tourism plans must target different types of attractions to different types of visitors. There are day visitors, convention attendees, business travelers, people visiting friends and family, vacationers, and niche groups from bird watchers to motorcycle clubs. They all spend money when they come to town. But they all want different services and amenities to cater to their particular needs and desires.

Approach your tourism plan as if you were designing a house. It should feature a welcoming entryway, all the necessary amenities such as bathrooms, a place to play, a place to relax, and a special room for each of your guests. If only Sarah Winchester had known — planning is the best method to keep the evil spirits at bay.

Questions for Success:
☐ Have you developed a business plan for tourism development and marketing?
☐ Do you know who your town's customers are and why they visit?
☐ Do you have a coordinated tourism effort?
☐ Does your tourism program tie to your economic development programs?
☐ Is there continuity in your marketing messages, materials and marketing theme?
☐ Are you seeing a good return on your investment in your tourism marketing and development efforts?
☐ Have you developed a plan with a good balance of product development and marketing?
☐ Is everyone on board? It takes a village to achieve ultimate success.

Rule 2

RELATIONSHIPS REQUIRE MORE THAN ONE PERSON

The rule of partnerships

What kind of "ship" never sails alone?

If you answered partner**ship**, then you have just recognized the most important rule in creating a successful tourism strategy. Partners are so important that it is impossible to even think that tourism programs can be successful when executed by a single entity. Take San Diego, California, for example. By partnering with an assortment of attractions — San Diego Zoo, SeaWorld, and even Disneyland, which is about ninety-five miles to the north — San Diego presents itself as part of the larger Southern California experience, worth traveling a longer distance to visit. Their strategy convinces millions of visitors to stay for a longer period of time.

In most communities, a single lead agency typically coordinates tourism development, promotion, activities, and events. It may be a visitor's bureau or the local chamber of commerce. But just because they are leading the charge does not mean they should do it alone. Tourism development and promotion must be a team sport, especially in smaller communities where resources are limited.

Partnerships accomplish a number of goals: they create continuity in the marketing effort, build a stronger brand for the community, reduce the duplication of efforts (multiple websites, toll-free numbers, etc.), and make "selling" the community easier. Prospective visitors are more likely to act when presented with a single vision, a single contact, and a single source for getting initial information.

There are three types of tourism partnerships, and all three should be developed.

- First, there are financial partnerships with other communities or tourism promoters, in which two or more — even all — of the partners pool funds to accomplish certain tourism objectives. This allows communities to leverage available funds for discounts on advertising, hiring public relations services, development of quality photo libraries, and first-class website development.

- The second type of partnership involves shared resources, which avoids the common duplication of services and visitor confusion. Imagine the benefit of shared photo libraries and press kits, single toll-free information request lines, etc.

- The third type of partnership involves leveraging the dollars and resources with private sector businesses. Quite often, the best attractions are privately owned. Work with them. Bring them into the program. Create public/private partnerships. For a guide, look at what San Diego and other successful tourist destinations have done.

Partners involved in tourism should include economic development organizations, convention centers, chambers of commerce, tribal units, cultural attractions and organizations, and event organizers, as well as city, state, or federal agencies. The more partners your town has, the more successful it will be. The biggest partnerships should be between communities, counties, or regions. Your town will always be much more successful as one loud voice, rather than a bunch of small voices.

Recently, the Washington State Audubon Society, a nonprofit organization, teamed up with three state agencies (Trade and Economic Development, Fish and Wildlife, and Department of Transportation), six communities, and the Bullet Foundation. Each organization had a role in providing technical, professional, or financial support. The final result was the creation of the first "Great Washington State Birding Trail."

Tourism partnerships are very much like a marriage. You agree, disagree, get upset, compromise, and then move on to a decision that will make all parties reasonably happy. The only difference is that in tourism, it's perfectly legal to have multiple partners, especially when you are building partnerships.

Questions for Success:

☐ Have you developed partnerships that include both public and private attractions?

☐ Is everyone on the same page in terms of your branding effort?

☐ Is there continuity in your tourism marketing and development efforts?

☐ Are you working closely with state agencies and taking advantage of other available resources?

Rule 3

PUT YOUR BAIT OUT ON THE HIGHWAY

The rule of billboards and exits

When people go fishing, they know that if they want to catch fish, they have to bring the right bait. Whether it's a distant shining object or a wriggling morsel, something must entice the fish to take notice and say, "Now that looks tasty."

People are not that different from fish. They need to be lured into your community. Billboards, highway signage, and other teasers are your bait. Offer people something tasty so they'll stop, linger, and spend money.

Billboards are brief marketing opportunities that need to grab drivers' attention and make them realize that what you're offering is what they need. It may be food, an attraction, an event, or even "the facilities." Simply stating that the exit leads to Our Town, founded in 1928, interests no one but you. (And, I'm not sure that even you really care when the town was founded.)

Use billboards to tell visitors why they should visit your town. Focus on things to do (visit the historical museum, take a winery tour, cruise the craft fair), things to see (world's biggest ball of waxed paper, smallest chainsaw carving), or places to eat (an ice cream shop, soda fountain, Italian restaurant, coffee shop). You get the picture. Now, make people who are driving by picture why they should stop for a visit.

The traveler may not even know what they want until they see your bait dangling from a billboard while driving past. But without that bait luring their attention away from the lonely road, they won't have a reason to take the exit into your town.

In order to be effective, highway signs must be presented in an eye-catching manner. There are four keys to success: use the right words, make it brief, keep the design simple, and keep the sign well-maintained.

Strong action words are the most successful draws to a community. Avoid worn-out or meaningless words like "welcome," "discover," "explore," or "we have it all." These signs seldom work because they don't give the visitor a reason to stop. You can only "discover" something once. The goal of your community-marketing plan is to keep people coming back time and again.

Promoting your town as a "gateway" is overused and used incorrectly. Gateways are something you drive through to get somewhere else. You want your town to be that somewhere else.

Make sure your highway signs are brief. People traveling at highway speeds have

---

While the billboard (opposite) is attractive, does it entice you to take the next exit? Does the event listed sell you on making a special trip back to Lovelock for Frontier Days? In promoting its casino gaming (below), Winnemucca played off the legend of Butch Cassidy who purportedly spent time in Winnemucca. The billboard provides a great teaser that will pique interest, is easy to read, has only nine words, and uses simple graphics.

approximately four seconds to read your message. If it's too much to read or too cluttered to grasp, the average traveler will simply ignore the sign. Have you ever turned to the person sitting next to you and asked, "Could you read all that?" or "What did that say?" The most effective signs include fewer than fourteen words. The best ones use fewer than ten. Fish won't bite if you hang half a dozen lures on the same line. In fact, they'll make a point of staying away.

Keep your signage and graphics simple. Most photos and graphic images are difficult to absorb from a distance. If a traveler has to spend all four seconds making out the graphic or photo, you've lost them. Magazine-style ads never make good billboards.

Finally, make sure that someone is assigned the responsibility of maintaining and updating the signage. Weeds and grass grow high when left unattended, and crucial information is often blocked from the view of speeding motorists. Do not expect the highway department to do this. Keep the signs up to date, there is no reason for motorists to stop in your town when the sign promotes an event that has already taken place. Highways are a community's front door. Welcome people with a well-manicured entrance and promotions of current activities. Make a good first impression.

Like fish, your potential visitors will be enticed by eye-catching bait that is too tempting to pass up. But, they won't bite at all unless you drop your line where the fish are swimming. In the case of tourism, this means out on the highways.

Here are two excellent examples: One simple graphic, few words, and easy to read from a distance. The "free wine tasting," using yellow on a black background, commands attention and creates a call to action. Both the museum and winery make it simple to find with easy to remember, simple directions.

Rule 4

TOILETS ATTRACT MORE THAN FLIES

The rule of necessity

"I gotta go." Those are the three most feared words heard by a parent on a long trip in the family car. You know it will be miles before you reach the next rest stop. It hasn't been that long since you passed the last one and asked the kids, "Do you have to go?" Of course, no one said a word. You press your foot down a little harder on the accelerator, hoping to make time pass quickly as your children begin to squirm in their seats.

Who would have ever thought that a small bladder would be such an important part of a community's tourism strategy? Restrooms are one of the easiest devices for luring visitors into your community. After all, you never know when the urge to go will cause them to stop.

Most state highway departments won't post signs for public restrooms other than rest stops, but if communities can promote the fact that they have them, they are sure to benefit from additional visitor spending.

You'd be surprised how a billboard with the words "Clean public restrooms — easy access" can translate into visitor spending. How? After you have used the facilities, have you ever said, "While we're here, why don't we look in that shop over there?"

Instead of saying "sorry, no public restrooms" or "for customers only" G. Willaker's in Wickford, Rhode Island has set a great example by letting customers know where the facilities are located. This creates additional spending in the community (the pharmacy with public facilities is a few doors down) and creates a sense of loyalty between the town and its customers.

Or, "While we're here, why don't we get something to eat?"

If your public restrooms also incorporate a visitor information kiosk, or are located next to an antique store, restaurant or attraction, the "facilities" can be surprisingly effective at bringing in customers. People like to stretch their legs a bit. They like the break. Your town needs to take full advantage of the most basic of human needs and the number one reason passers-by make unscheduled stops.

Businesses make a big mistake when they post signs stating that restrooms are for customers only. Most people don't even think about buying anything until they come out of the restroom. They will always empty the bladder before the pocket book. Prohibitive signs discourage visitors from becoming customers.

McDonald's doesn't offer public restrooms, but it knows that its restrooms are often seen that way. Every restaurant makes a priority of keeping its restrooms clean because their use typically translates into sales.

It's simple math. Imagine seven people crammed into a van on their way to a conference. After about one hundred miles, someone squirms uncomfortably and shouts, "Take the next exit. I see a restroom!"

What the person sees are golden arches. At the McDonald's, seven people pour out of the van. A couple of them go across the street to the Chevron Mini-Mart, and the rest enter the restaurant. Fifteen minutes later, they pile back into the van relieved of $40 spent on drinks and snacks to fuel them up until the next stop.

You'd probably be surprised at the sales volume mini-marts make as customers walk past the candy aisle and drink cooler on the way to and from the bathrooms. Or, maybe you aren't surprised because you are often one of those customers.

Multiply this one van by the number of vehicles that could be taking your off-ramp every day, and it can pay for a lot of toilet paper.

Smart communities have a profitable little secret when they provide people with the thing they need the most – restrooms. Located close to attractions or other visitor amenities with easy highway access, toilets will attract more money than flies.

The charming port town of Gig Harbor, Washington (population 6,500) has three public restrooms in various areas of its downtown. They also provide visitor information at each. They've got a captive audience and use it as an opportunity to encourage visitors to spend money while they're in town.

Questions for Success:
- ☐ Do you have restroom facilities available to visitors?
- ☐ If so, do you have signage letting them know they're available?
- ☐ Are your facilities close to places where those visitors can spend time and money?
- ☐ Are they well maintained?
- ☐ Are they easy to find?
- ☐ Is visitor information readily available?
- ☐ How do your restrooms stack up?
- ☐ Do they fairly represent your community in terms of cleanliness, curb appeal, etc?

Rule 5

FIRST IMPRESSIONS REALLY ARE LASTING IMPRESSIONS

The rule of perceived value

It may be true that we shouldn't judge a book by its cover, but it's also true that we do. Think back to your first moments with this book. Before even turning a page, you were already forming expectations about the level of quality you would find on the inside.

Each entryway into your community is the cover of its book. It provides the first hint about the character and quality of the people and businesses within your community. Make no doubt about it, your community WILL be judged by its cover.

Look at your community as a mall. You want visitors to come, spend time and money in your mall, then go home, tell friends how great it was, and come back often to visit again. The entrance to your mall is wherever you've posted the first sign that states "Entering Smallville" or "Welcome to Smallville." Take a critical look at your gateway signage to see if it reflects the community picture you want to project. Is the sign decorative, interesting, and easy to read? Or is it a typical aluminum street sign that is easy to ignore? Look at the landscaping, the lighting, and the businesses, or homes adjacent to the entryway. Does your entrance create a good first impression?

When you're on the road, hungry and want to take a meal break, how likely are you to stop at a drab building with a big sign that simply says EAT? Worse yet, how do you react to a restaurant with a sign that says CLEAN? Two things you want to assume about a restaurant: you can get food and the place is clean. If this were everything the restaurant owner could think to say about his establishment, you'd probably have to be very hungry, indeed, before you'd even consider stopping there.

On the other hand, if the building is painted and tidy, the landscaping trimmed and free of debris, has a cheerful appealing sign, and cars in the parking lot, you're likely to be eager to stop for a meal.

The same applies to lodging establishments, attractions, golf courses, and retail stores. If we're strangers in town and an establishment has not been recommended by someone, we make judgments based on appearance, because it's the only guide we have. The first impression will ultimately result in either "This looks like a nice place to stop," or "Let's keep going while we look for something more appealing."

Here are four important rules to creating a good first impression:

✓ Make sure that your entrance signs are in the right place. Most communities put them at the city or county limits, but that boundary has little or no marketing value. Because less desirable businesses and houses are often on the outskirts of town, placing signs there often paints a less-than-attractive picture of your community. Place your signs close to the action. Where people feel like the community begins is more important than government boundaries.

✓ Avoid sign clutter at town entryways. People don't need to see a listing of all your churches, service clubs and annual events on separate signs as soon as they drive into town. Find the right place for those types of signs around town and offer visitors a chance to stop and get more information about whatever interests them, but reserve

Example:
Based on the welcome sign (opposite) what is your impression of Borrego Springs, California? Does it look like a community you'd want to visit? It just so happens that Borrego Springs is surrounded by the incredible Anza-Borrego Desert State Park — the largest state park in the nation. The community offers several terrific golf courses, outstanding resorts (left), interpretive centers, and a shopping village. Often, well-meaning volunteer organizations develop these signs without realizing the negative impression they can have, which directly impacts the amount of money the community earns from visitors.

your entry sign to tell visitors why they should stop and stay awhile.

- Never list more than four items on your welcome sign and keep your verbiage to a minimum. People are in a hurry, so create signs with a message that can be quickly absorbed.

- Don't skimp on your town's welcome signs. Consider them an investment with a tremendous potential for return. Make sure the signs are attractive, professionally produced (sorry volunteers and local auxiliary organizations), impeccably landscaped with lots of color, lit at night, and cleaned and/or repainted once a year. Welcome signs and entry landscapes should be large, creating a "grand" entrance. They should be placed on both sides of the street or even span the street, if possible. Your "welcome" or "entry" should create a sense of arrival and make the visitor want to stop.

These same rules apply to businesses, particularly those in the tourism industry. In fact, as much as 70 percent of sales at wineries, golf courses, restaurants, lodging facilities, and retail shops come as a result of curb appeal — by creating outstanding first impressions, by making visitors want to open the covers of the book.

Why do you think residential subdivisions spend so much on their entries? It creates community pride (you want to live there), and increases the perceived value of the properties. Developers sell those properties faster and at increased values. The same applies with any community. Create a quality entry that proclaims the quality of your town and increases its perceived value. The greater the perceived value, the more visitors will spend, the longer they will stay, and the more likely they will come back.

For residents, perceived value translates to increased property values; stronger community pride; and the desire to live, work, and play in the community. A community can make an excellent first impression by just putting out an attractive welcome mat.

Here are examples of two lodging facilities. Where would you rather stay? Which one would you pay extra to stay in? Which of these two looks like a five-star hotel? If you picked the Mount Shasta Resort, you just made a decision based on curb appeal — your first impression. Most visitors would pay extra to stay there over an "ordinary" hotel or another facility in the area.

© Eric Sheckler

Rule 6

REAL MEN DON'T ASK FOR DIRECTIONS

The rule of wayfinding

In 1803, President Thomas Jefferson won approval from Congress for a visionary project that was to become one of American history's greatest adventure stories. Jefferson wanted to know if Americans could journey overland to the Pacific Ocean following two rivers: the Missouri and the Columbia.

It has been more than 200 years since Meriwether Lewis and William Clark made their historic 8,000-mile, 28-month trip. What makes their travels even more amazing is that they did it without any signs that said, "Scenic Body of Water This Way."

Most travelers today do not have the time or the patience to travel the lengths that Lewis and Clark did. Yet haphazard signage in some communities leads visitors into an unrecognizable wilderness, with no navigational aids to guide them. Signs should lead people to a destination, not cause confusion and irritation.

There are two primary signage issues that are critical to the success of any community: gateways and directional (or wayfinding) signage. Gateways introduce visitors to your community and provide a sense of arrival. Directional signs help visitors navigate through the area, while telling them what there is to see and do, where amenities are located (public parking, restrooms, visitor information, local services), and where the attractions are.

The second a potential customer exits the highway into your community they should have adequate signage to help them find amenities, services and attractions. These signs should be decorative and should fit the community's theme instead of being the standard aluminum municipal signage.

Developing a wayfinding plan should be a top priority to help you connect the dots through your community. Some communities have developed color-coded signage so that visitors can identify their next destination from a distance. As an example, public amenities might be in yellow, attractions in blue, and shopping areas in green. Signs should promote spending in your community, and can be a very powerful and effective selling tool.

Kingman, Arizona, is known as the "Heart of Route 66." The renowned cross-country route was made famous in the 1950s television show, the book Grapes of Wrath, and in countless songs (Get Your Kicks on Route 66). The city's new wayfinding program begins at the base of each freeway or highway exit and extends throughout the town. It not only plays up the theme, but also lets visitors know what the town has to offer and makes it easy for them to find the things that most interest them.

In the case of Kingman, four different types of signs were designed: entryway signage, banners along Route 66, directional signs (at each major intersection), and attractions signage (at the entry to each visitor attraction).

The journey that Lewis and Clark took was a difficult undertaking. Today's travelers are not looking for that type of challenge. Place your feet in the boots of those two historical trailblazers by identifying the quickest route from point A to point B and posting markers that show the way for those who follow.

Your "Wayfinding System" should promote your brand: what you want to be known for. Can you tell what the town of Leavenworth's theme or brand (below) is? One of the most popular destinations in the Pacific Northwest, Leavenworth, Washington, is a stunning Bavarian-themed town. Its signage reinforces its brand.

Newport, Rhode Island's wayfinding signage fits the nautical theme of this beautiful port city. If you happened to be visiting Newport and came across the sign (left) promoting the Oldport Water Taxi to Goat Island and Fort Adams State Park, would it pique your interest? Does it sound like a great activity?

Not only does wayfinding reduce traffic and make your attractions, activities and amenities more convenient, they also educate front-line employees about what your town has and where things are located. An attractive and professionally produced system is a great marketing tool that will increase sales.

Questions for Success:
☐ How easy is it for visitors to find the attractions, amenities, and services your town offers?

☐ Is your signage in keeping with the community's overall theme or ambiance?

☐ Does your town have an ongoing signage program in place?

Rule 7

20/20 SIGNAGE EQUALS $$$

The rule of perpendicular signs

As you drive into a town for the first time, your vision is automatically directed forward through the windshield as you attempt to make sure you don't violate local traffic laws or cause an accident. You are also trying to find your way around town. You may be looking for a place to park or checking out the town to determine whether or not there's any reason to stop. This keeps the driver looking primarily forward, rather than from side-to-side.

Most visitors are, arguably, pretty good at obeying local traffic rules. However, few people have the peripheral vision required to both drive and see what a town has to offer. That is, of course, unless the town and local retailers know the importance of perpendicular signage.

Many shops in a downtown district simply place their signs above the door or have them painted on windows. More often than not, these signs are missed by potential customers totally unaware of what they have to offer or that they even exist. Even driving ten miles per hour through town will make it difficult to read this type of signage while watching for pedestrians in unfamiliar surroundings. Remember driver's education? Eyes forward! Signs placed perpendicular to the building allow drivers to read them without turning their heads and can also be noticed from a further distance.

To further improve readability, the letters must be tall enough to see at a distance. The general rule for lettering is one inch for every 12 feet of distance. Letters eight inches tall can be read from 96 feet away, which is about right for a downtown core area with visitors traveling 15 to 35 miles per hour.

Pedestrians, too, will appreciate signs suspended over the sidewalk at a reasonable, consistent height. Have you ever had to crane your neck to figure out which store you wanted to enter because the signs were all displayed high atop the buildings? The Bavarian themed town of Leavenworth, Washington has done an excellent job of placing perpendicular signs that are easy to read by all visitors, whether they are in the car or on the sidewalk. The signs are decorative and in keeping with the town's theme. Perpendicular signs of uniform height and similar size are less likely to obstruct one another, are more pleasing to look at, and are more effective in bringing in customers.

A common mistake made by many retailers is not telling the visitor what the store sells. Visitors are not locals; the store names are irrelevant and typically meaningless to them. Often, they are looking for a certain type of store, such as a restaurant, gallery, antique, or toy store. No one will know that Kelly's Laffin Crab sells windsocks and kites, but the shop probably gets a number of people interested in eating shellfish. Your perpendicular signs should advertise the type of store — that's the lure that will bring shoppers inside — while the window or door should be used for the actual name. Sell what your town has, not what it is. This will greatly increase coveted drop-in shopping traffic.

Imagine what would happen if the highway department placed road signs parallel to the road, instead of perpendicular, or if they used only one inch tall lettering, or a script typestyle. They'd be largely ignored. Consider what works for them and apply the same sign design principles to downtown storefronts. Perpendicular signage allows motorists to keep their eyes on the road AND see what you are selling.

Rules for Success:

- ☐ Perpendicular, or blade signs should be consistent in height and size.
- ☐ Promote what you are selling not the name of the store. We know what Candlesticks (above) sells as a primary lure. We know the retailers in the top photo sell chocolate, collectibles, trains, and food.
- ☐ Create a call to action. Ice cream at the Presidents Information Center in Rapid City, South Dakota is a great reason to visit the center.
- ☐ Never use script text on signage and use no more than six words.

Rule 8

PARKING IS NOT JUST FOR LOVERS

The parking limits rule

Imagine that you have just been lured into a community's shopping district. It's a delightful place, and you can't wait to begin your shopping spree. You pull into a parking space, feed the meter, and soon discover that the stores were every bit as wonderful as you thought they would be.

Going from shop to shop, your credit card stays nice and warm from its constant use, as you buy gifts for your friends and, of course, lots of things for yourself. Before you know it, you end up spending hundreds of dollars in this great little town. You are so excited, you can't wait to get back home to show friends what you bought and share your experience with them.

You are soon walking back to your car, arms full of packages, reveling in the thought of coming back with your friends so they too can discover this gem. As you get closer to your car, you notice a slip of paper tucked under the windshield wiper. Immediately your joy turns to irritation. You got a parking ticket for exceeding the two-hour limit. Aargh!

Shopping and dining in a pedestrian setting is the number one activity of visitors across the country, and the one activity that generates the most amount of revenue for the community. It is the primary benefit of tourism. So why do communities discourage shopping and dining by restricting the time customers can stay? Many communities chase visitors away before they are done spending, and they do it for the wrong reasons.

Towns typically post two-hour parking limits so local retail employees will be forced to park elsewhere. Employers are unable to teach their employees the relationship between parking and shopping, so they have the city enforce an arbitrary deadline. Inadvertently, towns punish their customers because they can't get local workers trained to park elsewhere. Of course, this also punishes local businesses that could generate more revenues if they would just give their customers a chance to spend more time and money in their establishments.

Numerous studies have shown that shoppers — especially ones from out of town — take approximately four hours to satisfy their shopping and dining interest. Visitors forced to keep watching the time usually leave before they complete their spending. Rarely will visitors go out, feed the meter or move the car to another location, and then return to continue breaking out the plastic. Instead, they leave to spend their money elsewhere.

There are some communities that have discovered clever ways to help shoppers "shop 'til they drop." Spokane, Washington, a community that understands the importance of visitor spending, will put a "ticket" (opposite page) under the windshield wiper of cars in violation of the parking limit. To the shopper's delight the ticket states, "Thanks for visiting downtown Spokane. While you were enjoying incredible shopping, world-class entertainment, the region's best dining, or professional services, your parking meter expired. Don't worry! This courtesy parking ticket extended your parking privileges for an extra hour, allowing you to continue to enjoy your visit to Downtown Spokane."

Be sure to provide locations for RV and truck parking. RV travel is increasing by double-digit numbers every year, and these folks have higher-than-average disposable incomes and room to store lots of stuff. Don't put up signs that state "No RV or truck parking this block," without providing a solution: "RV and truck parking, next right."

If you insist on two-hour parking, then direct visitors to places where they can park for longer periods, four hours or more. Visitors will pay for parking if costs are reasonable and change available, but will leave if parking is expensive, restrictive, and hard to find.

A public parking garage in Covington, Kentucky, does it right. If you show receipts to the parking attendant that total $20 or more while you parked in the garage, the parking is free. Otherwise you pay the standard parking rates. People will spend more money than they normally would just to get free parking. Smart. Very smart.

Communities must recognize that the road to increased visitor spending and a vibrant downtown starts with plenty of tempting parking places with lots of time for spending. Successful communities will reap far more money from dollars spent in stores than from quarters spent in meters.

THANKS FOR VISITING

Nº 04173

DOWNTOWN
SPOKANE

While you were enjoying incredible shopping, world-class entertainment the regions' best dining or professional services, your parking meter expired. Don't worry! This courtesy parking ticket extended your parking privileges for an extra _1hr_ allowing you to continue to enjoy your visit to Downtown Spokane.

Date	Time	Meter N./Location
8 19 02	1 35 pm	3052

Lic. Plate	Lic. State/Yr.	Make/Model
044 JBX	Wa	ford

Veh. Color	Off.	Remarks
40435		

After this grace period, we ask that you move your car off this block or we will be forced to issue a parking citation.

We suggest utilizing off-street parking lots and garages for your long-term parking needs.

This courtesy has been made possible to you through the efforts of the Downtown Spokane Business Improvement District and the City of Spokane. Thank you for your continued support of Downtown Spokane.

White - City   Canary - BID   Tag - Customer

Making cents out of parking

Did you know that there are more than 6,000 off-street parking spaces Downtown?

If you work Downtown, or like to shop here often, there are alternatives to parking at the short-term meters that can save you time and money.

Downtown easyPARK

If you enjoy leisure time Downtown for shopping, dining out, or doing business, the EasyPark coupons from participating businesses are good for $1 off of parking lots, garages and transit. Ask your favorite retailer or business for EasyPark validation.

CITYTICKET
a better way to commute

CITYTICKET provides an cheap alternative r Downtown employees by providing ena parking and transportation to and m Downtown for only $19 a month.

information
EasyPark call
-0580.
CityTicket
28-RIDE.

DOWNTOWN
SPOKANE

Questions for Success:
☐ Do you have places for trucks and RVs to park?
☐ Do you have two hour (or shorter) parking limits that may be chasing customers away before they're done spending money in your community?
☐ Are your parking areas well signed, easy to find, and within a block of the downtown core area?
☐ Have you removed your parking restrictions after normal business hours?
☐ If you charge for parking, is change available? Is the cost reasonable?

Rule
9

THE BELLMAN DOES MORE THAN JUST OPEN DOORS

The rule of frontline sales

You just finished a wonderful meal in a community that you know very little about. Rather than immediately getting in your car and heading towards your destination, you decide to walk off your meal by exploring the downtown area and doing some window-shopping. You enter one of the shops and begin talking with the employee behind the counter.

You ask, "How is it going?"

"Fine" the employee replies.

"Business good?"

"Not really."

"Lived here long?"

"All my life."

"Anything exciting to do in town?"

"No. This is Mayberry."

Does this seem like the sort of place where you would want to spend much time? Unlikely. In fact, this employee not only lost a sale in this store, but also probably discouraged you from doing anything else in the town since there is nothing to do.

If, during the course of the above exchange, the employee engaged in any of the following behaviors: eye rolling, glaring, sighing impatiently, nursing a recent piercing, or ignoring you to discuss his or her love life with a fellow employee, you wouldn't even want to ask that person if there's anything to do. And, you wouldn't have anything nice to say about this community when you get back home.

Frontline employees are not just cashiers, stockers, wait staff, front desk personnel, or gas station attendants. They are also sales people for the community. In addition to making sales for the employer, they should sell events, attractions, and even the competition. Every dollar spent in the community will eventually become dollars in your pocket through increased tax revenues that will build parks, fix potholes, and encourage more visitors to your store for repeat spending experiences.

Frontline employees should be taught to ask three simple questions of their customers.

1. Where are you from?
2. How long will you be in town?
3. Have you been to... (or what brings you to town)?

These three questions will usually spawn a short conversation in which your sales person can promote a local attraction that fits the customer's taste. The longer you can keep a customer in town, the more likely that person will spend money there.

Huntsville, Texas, an historic town located about seventy miles north of Houston, has a clever attraction-adoption program created by town merchants. Each store promotes a different attraction to store visitors. This approach is much simpler than trying to train every frontline employee about every attraction or site in town. Additionally, by adopting one attraction, the staff can really get to know it, and can better promote it as a "must see" thing to do while visiting the area.

Frontline employees are a major part of the sales effort. Make sure they know how important they are; when they open the doors to your store, they also open doors to the community.

POINTS OF INTERESTS

ALLANDALE MANSION
BAYS MOUNTAIN PARK
EXCHANGE PLACE
FORT PATRICK HENRY DAM
HISTORIC CHURCH CIRCLE
NETHERLAND INN
RIVERFRONT PARK
WARRIORS' PATH STATE PARK

FOR MORE INFORMATION
CONTACT THE

Rule 10

KIOSKS NEVER SLEEP

The 365 and 24/7 rule

The primary objective of a visitor information center is to do exactly what its name implies: provide information to visitors. Typically, local chambers of commerce or convention and visitor bureaus are partially funded by lodging tax dollars, which visitors pay when they spend the night in the community. Hopefully, they are seeing some return on their investment in your community. Since a community never knows when a visitor will want information, the ideal VIC (Visitor Information Center) will stay open 365 days a year, 24 hours a day.

However, since the volunteers that staff most centers require occasional sleep, few are able to provide one-on-one contact with people who may be passing through town any time of day or night.

This is where the kiosk — typically a small structure that stays open 365 days of the year and never sleeps — comes in handy. Often made of wood, kiosks come in all sorts of sizes and shapes. They can be used to tell a story, or they can be used to promote events and attractions. Not only can they tell you where you are ("you are here!"), but they can also tell you where to go ("you can get there from here").

Install kiosks at several key locations that are easily accessible from the highway and primary thoroughfares. Work with the state transportation department to make sure that visitor information centers are given highway signage to direct visitors to the right location.

There are five keys to having a successful kiosk program in your community:

First, each should be able to withstand all sorts of weather. They are the mail carriers of tourism. They stay out in the rain, snow, and sleet. They deliver messages that people need in order to enjoy your community, and their messages promote the area, making it worth a longer stay or another special trip.

Second, kiosks should fit the character of the town. Communities that have themes or a well-known event or attraction should build the kiosk with that in mind. The kiosk then becomes not only a source of information, but also a marketing tool.

Third, they should be maintained regularly with current information about events and activities. Have volunteers remove expired events.

Fourth, the kiosk should also include a "take one" weather-resistant display rack offering a printed activities guide that visitors can take with them. Local and area maps should be available and plentiful. And remember, the kiosk is primarily for visitors, so avoid

EXAMPLES:

Kingsport, Tennessee, developed an excellent kiosk (opposite) that lists points of interest. Events are posted on the back side, and brochures are readily available 24/7. The kiosk blends in nicely with the historic brick architecture of downtown Kingsport.

Ashland, Oregon, offers visitor information in several places downtown, but when staff and volunteers have gone home for the day, information is still available (left).

making it a bulletin board for classified ads and local pancake feeds that have little or no interest to visitors.

Fifth, a town can never have enough visitor information sites. Convenience is critical. Not only should a kiosk be placed outside the doors to your visitor information center, but in other "stand alone" locations near your gateways and entrances to town. There should be one next to your public restrooms, in your shopping district, at major attractions and sites where they will cross-promote other sites. They should all have a similar look but be slightly different in the attractions they promote, have a user-friendly style, and include photographs and brief text selling the area attractions. Kiosks should be considered a sales tool and not just a location finder.

Kiosks should complement the volunteers that work at the visitor information centers, not replace them. They are not supposed to be substitutes for human contact. They are intended to be awake when your volunteers are asleep. As the famous Motel 6 slogan says, "We'll leave the light on for you."

Kiosks come in all shapes and sizes and can cost anywhere from a few hundred dollars to thousands. They can be free standing, or wall mounted. Each kiosk should be slightly different cross-promoting other areas, attractions, and amenities. Make sure they fit your brand and have room for brochures.

Rule II

CRITICAL MASS IS NOT JUST A RELIGIOUS EXPERIENCE

The rule of convenience

There are two types of retail stores in a community. There are neighborhood retail stores, which include hardware stores, professional services, taverns, pharmacies, grocery stores, and other shops geared primarily to local residents. Visitor retail, on the other hand, includes gift shops, galleries, bookstores, antique dealers, clothing stores, collectibles, restaurants, espresso shops, souvenir shops, and arts and crafts stores catering to both locals AND visitors. In some communities these are zoned separately but still convenient to one another.

If visitors want their shopping experience to be a real blessing and a truly religious experience, their best bet is to find a community that has visitor-oriented retail in a compact setting. This is what is referred to as critical mass.

You'll find that fast-food restaurants and gas stations congregate on all four corners of an intersection because they all benefit from the critical mass of having lots of convenient choices in one spot. People will spend more money in a community if they don't have to drive from one shop to the next.

The town of Sisters, Oregon, (population 1,500) was a dying timber town in the '70s until Black Butte Ranch, a neighboring resort, began its development. Knowing how the resort's guests would want a pedestrian-oriented shopping district nearby, the resort offered Sister's building owners the money to help create facades on the dated buildings in the core three-block area along the highway. Over the years, the town took on a new appearance (bottom photo, this page), and visitor-oriented retailers flocked to the newly designed shops. The neighborhood retail moved off the highway, because they didn't need the highway exposure any more.

The town of Chehalis, Washington, saw its many antique dealers congregate to a section of downtown, making the city the antique capital of the Northwest. By locating 30 or 40 stores together, it became convenient for visitors and locals alike to shop.

The same strategy applies to the success of outlet malls. Would you make a special trip to a community to visit its outlet stores knowing that the 30 stores were in different locations all over town? Would you feel differently if all of the stores were in a single location? Of course, you and millions of other outlet mall shoppers can attest to that.

By creating a critical mass of visitor-oriented establishments, towns can reap huge retail sales. As few as 15 visitor-oriented retail shops with dining and treats within a couple of blocks can spur very strong retail sales and can totally revitalize a town. Communities that develop a pedestrian-friendly, visitor-oriented retail village end up succeeding and know that critical mass can truly be a blessing.

How much is enough?

The minimum critical mass to create a destination downtown is the 10+10+10 rule. Within a two to three lineal block area (not square blocks) there should be at least:

- ☐ 10 destination retail shops (galleries, collectibles, home furnishings and accents, clothing, souvenirs, antiques (not second hand stores) books, etc.),
- ☐ 10 venues for dining and treats (restaurants, coffee shops, soda fountains, candy, bistros, etc.)
- ☐ 10 places open after 6 pm. Nightlife is critical, entertainment preferable.

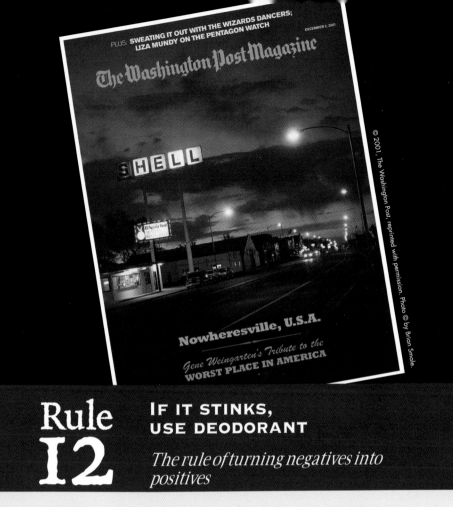

Rule 12

IF IT STINKS, USE DEODORANT

The rule of turning negatives into positives

The media have tremendous power in persuading people to do something or go somewhere. They provide movie reviews, restaurant ratings, and other commentary to help people enjoy themselves while spending their money wisely. More often than not, media reviews will have a positive impact on an establishment. However, if a community gets a bad review for a festival gone wrong, or if something negative takes place that is reported all over the country (or even in the region), its entire economy can be devastated.

It doesn't matter whether the information is correct or not. Once a negative comment is made, the story often takes on a life of its own, with little regard for its effect on the people who live in the area. However, a smart community with a bad review may find that it's not necessarily bad for business.

When the Washington Post designated Battle Mountain, Nevada, as "The Armpit of America" a small, friendly community suddenly became the butt of late night TV humor. Similarly, Highway 50, connecting five communities in Nevada, was referred to as "the loneliest road in America" in a LIFE magazine interview with a person from the American Automobile Association. He went on to say that people would need a survival kit if they were to get stuck there.

Certainly these comments did nothing to enhance the reputation of Battle Mountain or the communities along Highway 50. In fact, they dissuaded anyone from wanting to visit.

Rural tourism officials in Nevada met with these communities and decided that they could do one of three things: they could be mad and write letters to the editor and even cancel their subscriptions; they could let it go, hope that no one read the articles, and wait for it to go away, or they could turn a negative into a positive. As you might imagine, they agreed to the latter.

Folks in Battle Mountain now promote the "Festival of the Pit." Instead of an old-fashioned egg toss they stage a deodorant toss as part of the festivities. The chamber has even purchased a billboard on I-80 encouraging motorists to make a "pit stop" in Battle Mountain. It also sent a blanket invitation to any community that has been considered an armpit, they can have a free booth at the festival if they'll just show up and staff it.

Battle Mountain's stinky notoriety even landed them a sponsor for the event. Old Spice underwrites a portion of the activities. CNN and USA Today have covered the festival. And not only did USA Today run an article on the situation, they've offered to make bumper stickers saying, "Don't roll on by. Make Battle Mountain your next pit stop." Your town can't buy publicity like that. On top of all that, the community rallied together, and in just two weeks, hauled off more than forty tons of trash from around town. A major revitalization is now underway, and Battle Mountain has been seeing resurgence in its community pride, and in its tourism industry.

The Loneliest Road in America was another challenge for Nevada's tourism commission. A survival kit was created, promoted, and made available at retailers in every town along the route. It didn't take long before visitors from all over the country were exploring the loneliest road including the discovery of the "loneliest phone booth in America." Eureka, Nevada, now promotes itself as the "Friendliest Town on The Loneliest Road in America." All this publicity brings tens of thousands of people to the area each year. It is a good example of Yogi Berra's maxim that "Nobody goes there anymore. It's too crowded."

Being stinky and lonely may not be attributes that you would want to put on your town's résumé; however, a few choice hints to USA Today and CNN could turn that odor in the air into the smell of money rolling into your economy.

Questions for Success:
- [ ] What are the general perceptions of your community?
- [ ] Has your town had a visitor assessment?
- [ ] Have you taken a hard look at your town's challenges and how you might be able to turn those into assets?

Rule 13

INSANITY HAS ITS OWN REWARDS

The rule of being unique

How would you like to spend some time at the annual Mike the Headless Chicken festival in Fruita, Colorado? Or browsing in the gift shop inside a four-story high Brontosaurus near Palm Springs? Or how about attending the National Lentil Festival in the Palouse Region of Washington and Idaho?

They may not sound like the most exciting places to visit, yet tens of thousands of people flock to these communities every year to celebrate lentils and a chicken that supposedly lived for years without his head. People come from all over the world to shop inside a giant dinosaur's belly, feast on the largest pot of lentil soup, or participate in a great game of Chicken Bingo (the numbers are chosen by where the chicken droppings fall on a numbered grid.) What may seem rather insane to you means hundreds of thousands of dollars to the communities that came up with these zany ideas. For many people, being part of such silly fun is just too big an attraction to miss.

Coming up with an insane or unique idea does not mean that you have to be half-cocked in its development. It takes a great deal of planning and consensus in order to turn an idea into the theme that sets your town apart and makes visiting it worth a special trip. Your town's uniqueness may emerge in a variety of ways, such as architectural, event, or marketing themes.

A good way to start the insanity bandwagon is to look at the ideas of other communities. Don't copy them, but use them to inspire your own creative imagination. Let's say you start with Mike the Headless Chicken. We can agree that headless chickens are out – been there, done that. But maybe your community is the rubber chicken capital of the world ... or is rumored to have been the inspiration for The Headless Horseman ... or there was that flying pig incident back in the 1920s.

Riverside, Iowa, proclaimed itself the future birthplace of Captain James T. Kirk of Star Trek and began holding annual Trek-Fests. Hollywood and William Shatner played a practical joke on the whole town as a consequence, pretending to film a new movie there, and the town ended up with lots of publicity and a short series on Spike TV. Riverside's fame grew, and it's become a destination for Star Trek fans from as far away as Finland.

Along the Historic National Road in Illinois, travelers can gape at a 170 foot tall bottle of catsup, which is now in the Guinness Book of World Records. The City of Metropolis, Ohio, self-proclaimed hometown of Superman, boasts a 15 foot bronze statue of the hero, to the delight of thousands of comic book fans.

Americans may find comfort in the familiarity of a McDonald's on every corner, but they will seek out that which is truly unique. Sometimes it is as close as the nearest garage. A gentleman in St. Maries, Idaho, has collected every model Corvette ever manufactured, plus Corvette Indy pace cars. St. Maries has a timber heritage, but can you imagine the attraction if the whole town adopted a Corvette theme, with every store or restaurant adopting a model year, and, room permitting, placing one of the cars inside the store? Can you imagine the number of Corvette clubs, rallies, and classic car events that would gravitate to scenic St. Maries? Once there, visitors could learn more about St. Maries, including its timber heritage. The Corvette theme would be a powerful magnet. Much more so than, say, a timber museum.

A car museum is rather ordinary, but having the whole town adopt a Corvette theme with Corvettes in nearly every shop, would make St. Maries extraordinary.

In order to be successful in tourism a town must set itself apart from everyone else. If your community offers the same thing a visitor can get closer to home, then why should they make a special trip to visit your town? There really is no such thing as an insane idea. One man's headless chicken is another community's golden goose egg.

Questions for Success:
☐ What does your community have that makes visitors want to make a special trip, and that they can't get closer to home?
☐ What assets does your town have that could become the lure for visitors?

Rule 14

BE WORTHY OF A STANDING OVATION

The rule of being the best

Standing ovations typically take place in the theater, at a concert, or at an awards banquet. They are reserved for those people who have completed an excellent performance. A standing ovation is a spontaneous outpouring of appreciation for people who have truly done something outstanding in their craft. They are reserved only for the best.

Your community should strive to get a standing ovation from every person that visits. After all, the attractions, events, or amenities your town provides should exceed all others in quality. That makes your town worth a special trip. Why promote something that is good when your town can attract more people by being great? Offer the best and people will go out of their way to visit rather than choosing a similar experience that is closer to home. People have lots of choices when they travel. They have plenty of options for activities and attractions, and it is unlikely yours is the only community that provides a certain activity. Be different. Be great. Capture more of the visitor dollar.

There are 425 counties in the eleven western states of the U.S. Not surprisingly, every one of them — even in the urban areas — promotes outdoor recreation as a primary activity. Hundreds of counties and thousands of communities in these states promote

39

hiking, biking, horseback riding, surfing, snowmobiling, skiing, bird watching, or sightseeing. Many proclaim that they have it all. County after county continuously proclaims that they have hundreds of miles of hiking and biking trails. But if every county has the same thing, why should people make a special trip to a community farther away?

Case in point: Okanogan County is located in north central Washington, just below the Canadian border. Spectacularly beautiful with hundreds of miles of trails and year-round recreation, it still wasn't attracting visitors from the lucrative Seattle market. Why? The thirteen counties closer to the metropolitan area were promoting the same thing, so why drive an extra two hours to visit Okanogan County?

The folks in Okanogan Country scoured the guidebooks for quotes from people who have actually experienced the recreational activities there and began running ads using quotes they found: "Rocky Mountain powder in the Northwest? Go ahead, pinch yourself, you're in the Methow Valley." "Perhaps the best cross-country skiing on the continent." "Without a doubt, the best mountain biking in the lower 48." "A must visit destination for anyone, of any age, who owns or wants to snowmobile." Quotes like these now make Okanogan Country worth the extra drive.

People travel from around the world to ski at Whistler Resort in British Columbia. Why? Because it has been awarded the distinction of being the "Best ski resort in North America" for ten years running. In fact, Whistler, which will host the 2010 Winter Olympics, now does more business in the summer than during the ski season, making it a true year round destination.

Simply self-proclaiming that you're the best won't cut it. Your town needs third-party endorsements. Cozumel, Mexico, located in the Caribbean with hundreds of other legendary islands, was competing for a share of the lucrative scuba diving market, but had a hard time distinguishing itself from Aruba, Jamaica, the

Virgin Islands, Barbados, and countless other islands. That was until Cozumel was labeled the "drift diving capital of the world" by Skin Diver Magazine. This is now the thrust of Cozumel's marketing effort to the dive community. By being the best, and being recognized by credible sources as such, Cozumel has seen great tourism success.

Moab, Utah, is considered to have the best mountain biking in North America. Just hop on the web and search for "Moab biking" and you'll see thousands of links. It's not just a self-proclaimed title; enthusiasts, magazines, television documentaries, clubs, and a host of organizations have all bestowed the title on Moab.

Your town can't afford to rest on its laurels just because it is the best today. People are always gunning for the number one spot, and they'll take it away from you unless you do whatever it takes to keep your town on top.

Communities should develop attractions and supporting businesses that make them the absolute best. Your goal is to get all visitors to stop their cars on the way out of town, get out, turn toward the town, and applaud because your performance was so extraordinary.

Questions for Success:
- ☐ What does your community have that is better than what potential visitors can find closer to home?
- ☐ Have you searched for third-party endorsements in books, magazine articles, and other sources?

Rule 15

MOVIE CREDITS TELL THE REAL STORY

The rule of supporting businesses

Can you imagine buying a ticket to a movie where one person did everything? He or she was the star, the director, the producer, the grip, the casting agent, and even the best boy. It doesn't happen. There's a good reason why so many people work on a successful production. It's because no matter how big the star, no matter how good a job they do in marketing the show, the actor is nothing without a supporting cast and a team of technical experts. Filmmaking really is a team effort.

In successful tourism, there is never only one business holding up the entire industry. Not even Disneyland can do it alone. It needs airports, rental car companies, hotels, restaurants, and even other attractions that will keep people in the area longer.

Communities can develop an entire marketing campaign for their greatest attraction, but without supporting businesses, the attraction will never reach its full potential. Thirty years ago, Whistler Resort in British Columbia was just another rural community with about 750 residents and a dream. Whistler started as a seasonal ski destination, and most of the town's retail businesses couldn't survive the remaining seven months of each year. Then in the early 1980s, the development of the renowned Whistler Village began to take shape as a backdrop to the mountain attraction. Whistler Village is now home to nearly 200 retail shops, 85 restaurants, and 3,500 first-class accommodations. Additionally, there are mountain bike rentals, river rafting guides, two golf courses, and a host of other "supporting businesses." Even though Whistler is rated as the "Best Ski Resort in North America," it now does more business in the summer than in the winter months. Oh, the power of supporting businesses.

Not every community will have a mountain in their backyard, but most have attractions that are unique to the area. If hiking and biking trails are your claim to fame, seek out retail businesses such as bike rental, sales, and repair shops, tour guides, and supply stores. Sprinkle in a few restaurants and hotels that have lockers for bikes and gear, and you've got the makings of your supporting cast.

How do you find a supporting cast? The first rule of any business recruitment program is to ask your primary attraction, "What are the businesses that would help you be successful in bringing in more visitors or getting them to stay longer?" They will provide a list of suppliers as well as amenities and other attractions that will keep people spending money in the area for days, if not weeks. Primary attractions know the advantages of having their suppliers close by and a range of diverse activities available. They even appreciate competitors, knowing that the presence of one supports the other.

Communities also want to make sure that the supporting cast can be successful all year round. After all, being the best ski destination is only a four-month run. Whistler pioneers wanted the area to become more than just a winter resort, so their businesses could succeed. That is why you'll find the lifts open for mountain bikers and hikers during the off-season.

Whistler may continue to receive accolades as the number one ski destination in North America, but the supporting businesses are reaping the rewards of being profitable all year long.

Questions for Success:
☐ What are the biggest draws to your community?
☐ Does your town have the supporting businesses necessary to make those activities successful?
☐ Does your town promote the supporting businesses or just the activity?
☐ Does your town have a tourism/business attraction and retention program?
☐ Are your community leaders working with supporting businesses to promote your town's attractions and activities?

Rule 16

GREAT STORIES MAKE THE CAMPFIRE MEMORABLE

The rule of telling stories

The rancher's cattle were disappearing at alarming rates. A look at the dusty terrain did not uncover any human footprints, so they must not have been rustled. But carcasses weren't found either, ruling out wild animals. And since the fields were fenced, the Nevada rancher was quite sure the cattle didn't just wander off.

After months of agonizing losses, the rancher sent out a couple of farm hands to stake out the fields. They bedded down on a hilltop, and at dawn one morning, they heard loud whooping and hollering and the sounds of bellowing cattle in the valley down below. They scrambled out of their sleeping bags and ran down the hill as fast as they could to where the cattle were gathered. With guns loaded and cocked, they stopped, dead in their tracks, gaping in amazement...

Storytelling has been a form of entertainment since the Stone Age. It began with stories around the campfire and etchings on the cave wall and has progressed to bedtime stories and midnight readings of Harry Potter. Storytelling, like opposable thumbs, is a characteristic that distinguishes humans from all other animals. Stories entertain, teach, establish moral precedents, and recall our genealogy. They can do just about anything and always bring people together — including bringing visitors into a community.

Cultural tourism is the fastest growing segment in the tourism industry. It takes visitors on a journey of discovery, beyond the gift shops and amusements and into the community's soul, into its history, environment, and the arts.

Museums are a mainstay of cultural tourism. They will often display items from the town and showcase some of the unusual characters that lived there. But many museums fail because they simply show artifacts rather than tell stories. They have collections of old bottles, typewriters, furniture, industry equipment, and all sorts of memorabilia that have meaning but no context.

What makes a museum successful is its ability to tell stories, either oral, written or visual. An artifact without a story is boring to most people. But a story brings it alive. It makes it real and memorable. And it keeps visitors in the community longer, which translates into more spending. Museums that tell great stories will captivate visitors for hours, and they'll develop a bond with the community. Best of all, they'll tell other people, who more than likely will have to see it, read it, or hear it for themselves.

And now, for the rest of the story:
...they stopped, dead in their tracks, gaping in amazement as they came face to face with the old crook, Crazy Tex Hazelwood, rustling the rancher's cattle while wearing the novel shoes you see here (below right).

Want to see, read, and hear some more great stories? Visit the Northeastern Nevada Museum in Elko. But beware; you'll be there for hours.

Questions for Success:
- ☐ Do your town museums tell stories or just display artifacts?
- ☐ How long does the average visitor spend in your museum(s)?
- ☐ Are the stories interesting enough to capture the visitor and entice them to return?
- ☐ Are the displays unique and captivating?
- ☐ Are interesting stories about local buildings or sites included as part of the museum program?

Rule 17

THE SHORTEST DISTANCE BETWEEN TWO POINTS IS A GOOD TIME

The Four-Times rule

If you live in a rural area and need to make periodic trips to the big city, do you develop a mental list and run a number of errands while you are there? Sure. You are making it worth the drive by getting more done and saving precious time. You certainly don't want to spend more time in the car than you do in the shops.

When it comes to tourism, people determine their trips the same way. People will visit your community if it has activities that interest them, and that will keep them busy four times longer than it took to get them there. So if you expect a visitor to drive fifteen minutes to see your town, it will need to have at least an hour's worth of activities in order to make it worth the drive. This is referred to as the Four Times Rule.

If your community is located an hour from the major population area from which you are trying to attract visitors, it needs to have four hour's worth of activities that cater to that visitor.

Planners and builders often utilize this rule when making their decisions on where to locate facilities. For example, when a movie theater decides on a location, knowing that most movies are about two hours long, they look at the population within a 20- to

30-minute radius. Few people will travel more than twenty minutes just to see a movie, unless it is combined with other activities such as shopping or dining.

The Four Times Rule will determine your town's major market area. The more you have to offer and the more powerful the draw, the farther people will travel to visit. Look at Branson, Missouri, with its 49 music theaters. It's a national draw and keeps a majority of its visitors busy for days.

The Four Times Rule also determines whether or not your town can become an overnight destination. To lure overnight visitors to your primary attractions, your town needs to have at least eight hours of activities that will cater to the visitor. Your community must also have the other amenities that go with overnight stays such as lodging, dining, entertainment, and supporting businesses.

The ultimate goal of a community with a focus on tourism is to become worthy of multi-day and repeat visits. After all, overnight visitors spend three times more money than day visitors. Areas that create overnight stays are worthy of a special trip. You may have heard of a few of these: Orlando, Branson, Hawaii, Disneyland, and Yellowstone National Park.

Let's say you really need a break, highly unlikely, but let's just pretend. Would you buy (at regular prices) a ticket to Hawaii, leave Saturday morning, get there late Saturday, and then come back Sunday afternoon in time for work Monday morning? Chances are, you'd probably call in sick or take some additional vacation days to make it worth the trip. This is why the average stay in remote locations, like Hawaii, is typically a week or longer.

The same rationale works for smaller communities as well. What makes visiting your town worth the drive? Does your town have enough attractions to become a destination community?

Traveling in cars and planes used to be fun and exciting, but lately it has become much more time consuming and uncomfortable. Communities need to create an environment that people will look forward to, where the pleasure of community activities and attractions outweigh the discomfort of travel. Only then will people remember that the quality of the visit outweighed the length of time it took to get there.

Questions for Success:
- [ ] Have you taken a look at your town's activities and their drawing power?
- [ ] Have you determined who your town's major markets are?
- [ ] Does your town have the activities that make visiting it worth the drive?
- [ ] Have you explored how you use the Four Times Rule to attract more visitors?

Rule 18

HAPPINESS IS POSITIVE CASH FLOW

The rule of marketing versus product development

Cash flow is the lifeblood of the economy. The goal of every business is to have enough cash coming in so that it can pay the bills and improve what it has to offer. As long as more money is coming into the business than is going out, people are happy. The benefit of tourism is that it is an import industry. Visitors come into town, spend money, and go home, which imports cash into the local economy. Successful communities import more cash from visitors than they export from residents who earn money locally and spend it elsewhere.

A goal of just about every community is to effectively promote their attractions and events and help keep their businesses in positive cash flow. The more money that goes into effective promotion, the more local businesses will reap as a result of visitor spending. The more money a business makes, the greater the tax collections that go back to the community. The more money the community collects, the more money that is available to use on community promotions. Thus, the cycle continues, always improving the business climate and opening up opportunities for new and growing businesses.

While the marketing effort is important, it should not be the only priority.

Many communities make this mistake, when they should also be investing in upgrading or adding to their product. If a business puts all of its money in advertising and little or nothing into inventory or product development, the business will ultimately fail. Quite often, travelers will visit a community as a result of the marketing effort and go home disappointed, never to visit again. For others, when it comes time to plan the next trip, they will cross your town off the list as a "been there, done that" community. Others won't be convinced that your town has enough to offer to make a special trip in the first place, and some travelers will simply know better.

The point is that every single community should make product development the top priority. Activities. Attractions. Amenities. Always invest in product development first and marketing later. A smart community will initially spend 90 percent of its available tourism budget on product development, and as the product gets better and better, gradually tip the scales to perhaps 50 percent product development and 50 percent marketing.

While every community is different, the scales should never be tipped to more than about 70 percent for marketing. Product development never ends; it's an ongoing process and should ALWAYS be the priority. Remember, people visit your town because of the product(s) it offers. Keep adding to it and making it better, and you'll get more repeat business, have a longer season, and a strong brand that will require less effort to market.

The product development budget should not be spent solely for community events and attractions that draw visitors. Your town must also invest in signage, wayfinding, visitor information kiosks, public restrooms, theme development, beautification, supporting businesses, and so forth. Communities must also make sure that they talk to their business owners and learn what infrastructure should be upgraded or developed to help enhance their community — the product — and keep people coming back. This is part of a business retention program. Without a strong business retention program to support local businesses, a tourism program will never succeed.

A good product successfully marketed will result in continued cash flow that will keep businesses and the community happy.

Rule 19

SELL THE RAPIDS, NOT THE RIVER

The rule of selling the experience

One of the most spectacular places to river raft in the Pacific Northwest is along the Skykomish River, near the little town of Index, Washington. A spot along the run is called Boulder Drop, and many guidebooks rate it as a four on a scale of one to five. A five rating is the most treacherous. What makes it remarkable is the clear blue water that allows you to see to the bottom of the river, followed by a sudden rush of frothing white water rushing around huge boulders and dropping off into ten-foot waterfalls, which you attempt to navigate around and through. The ice-cold water slaps you in the face as you try to navigate the raft toward the next spot of calm water without capsizing and leaving stranded rafters floating down the river or hanging onto the huge boulders.

As you tighten your grip on the oar while attempting to see through the water in your eyes and hear the laughter and screams of your friends (mainly screams), all thoughts leave your mind. You're in the moment, living only for that rush of adrenaline.

The next time you think about Index, you will probably remember Boulder Drop and the excitement and the cool mist on your face; you won't care whether the town was named Index or Thumb or Ringfinger.

All too often, communities get stuck promoting the place and not the activities. Visitors are far more interested in the things to do than in the location. People will travel farther to feel the rush of 40-degree water splashing over them than to visit a quaintly named town that sounds a lot like quaint towns closer to home.

County marketing groups are notorious for promoting the county as a destination. Have you ever gone anywhere because it was a county? Would you prefer to visit the world-renowned Napa Valley or Napa County? Napa County sounds like a government entity, while Napa Valley sounds like a beautiful place to see and visit. The Napa Valley is widely known as Wine Country, which truly gets to the heart of the experience, and why it is known worldwide.

How do you make the experience tangible for someone who is still sitting at home in his or her armchair? One of the least expensive channels is the Internet. Brief, eloquent descriptions of your surroundings, accompanied by professionally shot photographs and third-party reviews will lead visitors to the water and make them grab the nearest raft. As high-speed connections become the norm, action-packed short movie clips (it only takes a few seconds) delivered over the Internet can bring activities to life and make visitors want to go there.

One of the most popular forms of promotion is the development of an activities guide rather than a standard brochure. An activities guide is a multi-page booklet or brochure that dedicates at least one page to each major activity or attraction. Too many brochures provide only lists of things to see and do, when photos and descriptions selling the experience would be a more effective lure. The more your town

has to offer, the longer people will stay, and the more likely they will return. Even using the simple words "activities guide" tells a potential customer that your town has things to do. The word "brochure" says nothing. Would you be more likely to "call for your free brochure" or "call for your free Activities Guide to the Northwest's Best River Rafting?" We all want things to do, not just things to see.

Effective tourism marketing revolves around two words: Evoke emotion. The thrill of the roller coaster; the relaxing, serene feeling of sitting on a quiet beach at sunset; or screaming at the top of your lungs as your raft spins sideways and drops down over the waterfall. Once you can effectively sell the experience, people will flock to your location.

Welcome to the "Experience Economy," recently outlined in a book of the same name by authors B. Joseph Pine and James H. Gilmore. Their premise is that work is theater and every business a stage. We might take that even further and say that every town is a stage, and to become a destination, you need the screenplay (your brand) and the actors (local businesses and events).

More than ever before, visitors want things to do, not just things to look at. They want to be immersed in music and culture, the environment, recreation, history and even food.

Pay a visit to Plimoth Plantation (left), located along the Massachusetts Atlantic coast, where "actors" live, work, cook, and speak as they did when the first pilgrims stepped off the Mayflower.

Questions for Success:
☐ Is your town selling activities or places?
☐ Does the text in your town's marketing materials evoke emotion?
☐ Do your town's marketing materials simply list activities or does it tell visitors why they should take part in those activities?

Rule 20

MAKE IT EASY TO TELL YOUR COWS FROM MY COWS

The rule of branding

The Romans used brands as symbols to identify their professions. A row of hams depicted the butcher's trade, a cow symbolized a dairyman, and a boot reflected a cobbler. The markings represented crafts rather than specific craftsmen. Soon after, Romans began using their brands to advertise themselves, while the Egyptians seared insignias into livestock to identify their stray or stolen animals. This latter custom was passed on to ranchers and became the symbol of ownership in a business where ownership was everything. Branding became such a big part of a rancher's life that they used to say that a good cowboy could recognize and understand the Constitution of the United States if it were only written with a branding iron on the side of a cow.

Branding your community is the process of setting yourself apart from everyone else. Your town's brand should be pervasive throughout the community – your wayfinding system, gateways, all community-related websites, brochures, experiences, and photography should reflect the brand. Using successful tourism strategies, communities create a subconscious association with the brand so that visitors picture a place they would like to visit whenever they see the brand.

A brand must be obvious in your marketing and in your town. When visitors arrive, do they see your brand throughout the community? When you arrive in Hershey, Pennsylvania, you'll notice that the street pole lamps are shaped like Hershey's kisses, reinforcing their brand as the chocolate capital of the world.

The brand association may involve any or all of the senses. In a society that's information rich and time poor, people value feeling more than information. Branding creates the perception a potential visitor has about you. When you hear the word "Disneyland" you may picture mouse ears, the Matterhorn, and Goofy, and automatically associate it with fun, fantasy, and families. You really don't think of Anaheim, where Disneyland is located. Disneyland is the "brand" associated with the city. That's what people remember.

People familiar with the garlic festival in Gilroy, California, may have an olfactory or gastronomical sensation upon hearing about that event. And everyone knows that "Virginia is For Lovers," according to a long and successful campaign.

Branding is NOT just slogans and logos. Brands are what people think of your town's product (attractions, activities), not what your marketing materials say about them. Do you go to Disneyland because their slogan is "the happiest place on earth"? Of course not. You visit the popular theme park because of what you know about it. Perceptions — much of it developed by word of mouth — are the key to developing a brand. The slogan simply reinforces your perceptions. Disneyland is a great place for kids and family and the slogan reinforces the perception that it's the happiest place on earth. Employees are trained and re-trained to make sure the Disney parks deliver on that promise.

Brands are about product more than marketing. Las Vegas would be in trouble if it was touted as America's adult playground but didn't have the strip, the mega-resorts, and dozens of shows and casinos. "What happens here, stays here" might not work for Muskogee, Oklahoma.

Successful brands are never generic. This is the age of specialization. Find your niche and work to own it. "We have something for everyone" will not get anyone to visit you. We all want something for me; we don't care about everyone. Notice the "Words to Avoid" on the next page. Be specific, fun, colorful, weird, scary, silly, adventuresome, or lazy. But don't be generic. The more generic you are, the less likely visitors will pick your town over others as a place to visit.

Brands rarely succeed as a top-down effort. The most well branded communities were all grass-roots efforts, privately developed. The city is there to assist. A perfect example might be Branson, Missouri. This town of 6,500 residents hosts 7.5 million visitors a year. Its brand "The Music Theater Capital of the World" is founded on the 49 privately developed theaters in Branson, and the stars who occupy them: Andy Williams, The Osmonds, Boxcar Willie, Jim Stafford, and dozens of others. Branson helps market the brand; it didn't create it.

The real trick to branding is to separate your primary lure from your diversions. The primary lure is the experience or activity that separates your town from everywhere else. Diversions are the secondary activities, things you can do closer to home but will do while you're in the area. What makes Branson truly unique are those 49 theaters.

They are Branson's primary lure. Diversions include outlet malls and shopping, dining, golf, fishing, boating, a multitude of outdoor recreational activities, water parks, and other attractions, and dozens of restaurants. But even though Branson has something for everyone the brand is the Music Theater Capital.

While no one wants to be classified as a diversion or secondary activity, consider the following: Visitors are active 14 hours a day, yet typically spend only four to six hours a day with the primary lure that brought them to town. In Branson, the average visitor will see two shows a day (four hours total), and then they spend eight to ten hours with diversionary activities. In fact, a full 80 percent of visitor spending takes place with diversions. Would you go to Orlando if Disneyworld were not there? If you said no, you just slammed Universal Studios. Do they mind being a diversion? Of course not, because a full three quarters of the people going to Disneyworld also visit dozens of other attractions while there.

Branding a community is not an easy strategy to undertake. In the first place, it requires the varied disciplines of business, product development, marketing, communications, and graphic design. Second, it requires buy-in from the community in order to send a consistent message. Third, it takes time. Communities that are in a rush to get their brand known will inevitably fail as a result of poor planning and inadequate feedback. Budweiser didn't become the King of Beers overnight.

Building a brand requires a concerted public relations effort. Public relations is used to build the brand, while advertising maintains your position once you're on top. The branding process may include repositioning (for communities turning themselves around), image (defining who your town is), market definition (defining who your town hopes to attract), creation of an icon (the photo opportunity), and finding your town's niche (defining the unique feature that will attract visitors).

Tourism is not the first industry to try to brand itself for market share. Companies have been doing it for centuries, and communities are finally getting the idea. If you want customers to choose your community when there are dozens of communities closer to home, you'll need to let them know the difference between your cows and the cows next door.

Words and phrases to avoid:

- Discover
- Best kept secret
- Historic downtown
- Something for everyone
- The four season destination
- So much to see and do
- Explore
- Outdoor recreation
- We have it all
- Visit (name of town)
- Unlike anywhere else
- So much history
- Gateway
- Center of it all
- Naturally fun
- Experience
- Next to everything
- Come visit us

Questions for Success:

☐ What do you have that clearly sets you apart and that you can build your brand around?

☐ Are your local organizations on the same page in terms of developing your brand?

☐ Do your events follow the marketing "theme" you are trying to build?

Rule 21

PHOTOS ARE WORTH A THOUSAND NIGHTS

The rule of "wow" photography

Nothing sells tourism as well as photography. The use of outstanding photography should truly sell the experience. The picture of a resort is nice, but what makes the sale is the photo of guests playing tennis or lying by the pool. People are looking for experiences, things to do, activities. Don't show the river, show the kayakers. Don't show the water slides, show the fun. Your photos should evoke emotion; they should make a potential customer say, "Wow. I want to go there," or "That looks like fun!"

Brochures and advertisements are the most expensive parts of any tourism strategy. You want to provide enough information to guide people to the next steps: making plans and making reservations. Too much text and you'll lose your audience. Photographs are a way to tease people, to pull them into your ad, article, or activities guide. They are a way to say, "This could be you climbing or hiking or getting that relaxing massage."

Every community should develop a professional photo library with between 60 and 100 photographs. They should showcase every season, and at least 75 percent of them should feature people enjoying activities. While scenic vistas may create ambiance, in reality, they capture the visitor for only a few minutes. Your goal is to entice people to come and spend money in the community, not stop for a minute, look, and then leave.

The best way to begin your search for photos is to go to a bookstore and look at the numerous pictorial travel books that feature your area. You will generally see books that are filled with stunning photography. Look at the credits and make contact with the photographer(s) to ask if you can use some of their photos to promote the area.

Another way to find photos is to identify the professional photographers in your region and tell them that you want to promote the area with highlighted events and activity photos. It will be easy to distinguish between those that take wedding and graduation pictures and those that take action shots.

Costs can vary, but expect to pay for quality work. Think of this as an investment. Every person that looks at photos of your community could be spending some money as a result of the picture you choose.

Expect to negotiate with the photographer. This is their work, and they take great pride in it. They not only want to make sure they are compensated fairly, but also that the photos are presented correctly. Most photographers will retain the rights and limit your use. You should expect to professionally digitize the photos in a large, high-resolution format. Anything else will diminish their quality.

Many communities make a limited number of high-resolution photos available on their websites for use by the media. Working on deadline, a publisher may discover a hole that needs filling after regular working hours. You can be a hero to the editor and improve the odds that a story about your community will be seen and read by offering 24-hour access to online photos. Some websites require registration before downloading photos to discourage inappropriate distribution of these professional images.

Some communities will seek to have photos taken by amateurs. Some even hold periodic photo contests. Though these photos can be kept in the library and displayed at community events, they rarely meet the professional standards required for marketing materials. Remember, these photos will be used to entice people to come and stay in your community. They must have "wow" appeal.

Photos are not only worth a thousand words; if they get people to stay for several days, your photos will be worth a thousand nights. Room nights, that is.

Questions for Success:
☐ Have you budgeted for the development of a photo library?
☐ Does your photo library include activities more than scenic vistas?
☐ Do your photos have "wow!" appeal?
☐ Have you looked at other ads, brochures and/or websites to see what a difference good photography can make in closing the sale?

Rule 22

DON'T LET YOUR LAST OPPORTUNITY BECOME A LOST OPPORTUNITY

The rule of closing the sale

Newspapers, brochures, magazines, special events, direct mail, trade shows, the Internet, television, radio, transit advertising, billboards, dioramas — these are just a few of the tools and outlets that companies use to get people to buy their products. People are bombarded hundreds of times every day with someone trying to sell them something. Watching television for just one hour will expose you to nearly fifty commercials. Looking at a magazine or newspaper may expose you to twice that amount. The bottom line? Your marketing materials MUST be good enough the close the sale. Each piece may be your last opportunity to convince a potential visitor to pick you over the next destination or event.

An excellent advertising or PR program can get potential visitors to call for your "free activities guide" or get them to log on to your website, but both better be good enough to close the sale. Otherwise, your marketing dollars are largely wasted.

There is an old saying that "I know that half my advertising dollars are wasted. The problem is I don't know which half." It's not really very funny if you're the one spending the money. Most communities waste more than 85 percent of their marketing dollars because they fail to understand how to market effectively. That's right, 85 percent. Pick up a magazine or the travel section of the Sunday paper. Look through the travel ads. Which ones are good enough to get you to make a call or log on to a website? Then, when you get the brochure or look at the website, which places entice you to visit?

Every community promotion, regardless of the medium, should do two things: First, it must create a positive image of your community. People want to visit places that are reputable, that seem like a nice place to go. Visitors want to see and experience events and attractions that are highly regarded, either by word of mouth or by objective third parties. It's not necessary to use a lot of text. Short quotes from recognizable people will go a long way toward bringing customers to you.

Second, there must be a call to action. This spells out the next step and often provides an incentive: "Call for our free Activities Guide to the Best Snowmobiling in the Lower 48," or "Take a virtual tour at www.ourtown.com." It must take the reader to the next step: either getting them to call for more information, log on to the website, or make those plans and reservations.

Do the words "Welcome to Fredonia, NY" make you want to pick up this brochure? What picture comes to mind when you hear about Fredonia? If you're not from the area, the town's name means little.

Just for fun, we picked other words for the cover of the brochure and focused on selling the ambiance, the brand, the experience. When you hear the words " A picturesque Victorian village set among the vineyards of Western New York," does the town sound more appealing? Perhaps a place you'd like to visit? Would this entice you to pick up the brochure if you were planning on visiting nearby Niagara Falls?

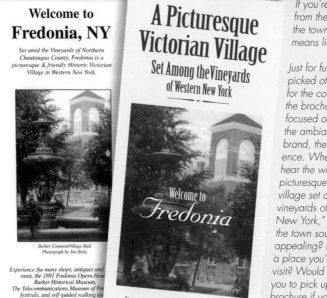

Welcome to Fredonia, NY

Set amid the Vineyards of Northern Chautauqua County, Fredonia is a picturesque & friendly Historic Victorian Village in Western New York.

Barker Common/Village Hall Photograph by Jim Boltz

Experience the many shops, antiques and restaurants, the 1891 Fredonia Opera House, Barker Historical Museum, The Telecommunications Museum of Fredonia, festivals, and self-guided walking tour.

Fredonia...Timeless...Treasures
Relax in a Gracious Victorian Village

A Picturesque Victorian Village
Set Among the Vineyards
of Western New York

Welcome to
Fredonia

Experience the many shops, antiques and restaurants, the 1891 Fredonia Opera

When developing brochures, make sure you use contrasting colors. From a distance would you be able to read Red Sky at Night's Sailing Adventures brochure? We did a very quick makeover, making the experience bold and yellow on the contrasting dark background. Note: Always sell the experience before the name of the business (Red Sky at Night Sailing Adventures is the name of the business). Promote Sailing Adventures and then elevate Kootenay Lake by using a superlative such as "stunning." Then promote why you're the business to pick once they pick up the brochure. Would you notice the made-over brochure from a distance? Does it sound like a fun experience?

The top two to three inches of your brochure, activities guide, or ad must grab the reader's eye, while the bottom should have your potential customer grabbing for the phone or a pencil in order to write down the number or website address.

Tens of thousands of communities spend more than $2 billion each year in the U.S. alone trying to get visitors to their community. That's a lot of marketing! The competition for the tourist dollar is tremendous and growing as more and more communities try to entice visitors to their town.

In the race to win people's vote as the place to spend their precious time off and spend their hard-earned travel money, second place doesn't count. Your town is either chosen or not. Winning marketing programs can create winning communities.

Questions for Success:
- [ ] What was it that convinced you to book your last vacation trip?
- [ ] Are your marketing materials good enough to close the sale?
- [ ] How do your materials stack up to other communities' marketing materials?
- [ ] Are the top three inches of your brochure good enough to capture the attention of a potential customer?
- [ ] Do your brochures sell activities (things to do not just see)?

odger Tamblyn/Alamy

Rule 23

BRAGGING IS MORE EFFECTIVE WHEN SOMEONE ELSE DOES IT FOR YOU

The rule of public relations

Oyez, Oyez (roughly translated as "hark" or "listen") became a familiar call in town squares, markets, and public meeting places all over Britain in the 1700s. Town criers used those words to summon the townspeople to gather and listen to news of plague, victories in far-off lands, royal births, and deaths by execution.

Criers were usually people of some standing in the community, as they had to be able to read and write the proclamations. The crier would read a proclamation and inform the public of matters of importance. They were considered the first "talking newspapers," but in reality they were the mouthpieces that promoted the king's actions and programs. In modern times, we call them public relations people, but their duties are still the same: to promote the client from a third party's viewpoint, and to spread the word.

Public relations is a vital and very important, but often overlooked, complement to advertising. Studies show that 10 percent of vacationers choose their trips as a result of ads they see, 40 percent as a result of an article they have read, and 50 percent because of word-of-mouth recommendations made by friends or family.

Together, advertising and public relations can easily account for more than half your visitor spending, and it's important to have a balance between them.

With advertising, you pay for the privilege of seeing your message run in a guaranteed position, exactly as you wrote it. With public relations, the route is less direct. You suggest a good story to an editor and hope it will be picked up by the news media, trade publications, and websites. The cost is always lower, but you have less control over the final message. You pay for advertising, you pray for good PR.

Given the relative lack of control, why is public relations so successful? Credibility. A magazine may publish an article that you have provided, verbatim, but to the reader there is an appearance of objectivity. Public relations generates a third-party endorsement, while in advertising you're tooting your own horn. Moreover, articles are three times more likely to be read than paid ads. People subscribe to the local paper and magazines for the articles not the ads.

Some people think PR means sending out a few press releases. A good public relations program goes much, much farther, establishing relationships with editors and sometimes creating stories — and attention — where none existed beforehand.

Paying a professional public relations firm to place articles in targeted outlets should be a priority and is always cost effective. Print, radio, and television ads can cost an enormous amount and must appear regularly in order to be effective. In comparison, public relations offers a greater return on investment. Some studies have shown that $3 of publicity (referred to as earned media) is attained for every $1 spent on a public relations campaign.

Bragging about your community is fine as long as you let others do it. Some communities may decide that it is time to bring back the town crier who can act as an ambassador, deployed to draw attention to special events and attractions in your area.

Oyez, oyez, oyez.

Third-party endorsements are the most powerful motivators. That includes word of mouth, non-biased articles and endorsements. If you have them, use them. If not, develop a PR program.

Rule
24

LET YOUR FINGERS DO THE WALKING

The rule of websites

Back in the 1960s, the phone company developed a marketing campaign that encouraged people to use their product more. "Let your fingers do the walking" became synonymous with picking up the yellow pages and finding a business. People still let their fingers to do the walking, but they are more likely to be found on a keyboard than on a dial pad.

Consider the following:

✔ A new website goes online an average of every three seconds.

✔ More than 64 million travel-related domain names have been registered so far.

✔ The Internet is fourth only to electricity, the automobile, and television in its influence on daily American life.

✔ Seventy-five percent of all Americans use the Internet regularly, and sixty-eight percent have immediate access to the web either at home or work.

- New Internet users are growing at a rate of nearly ten percent per month!

- Ninety-four percent of all Internet users plan their travel using the web.

Website use for travel planning has grown incredibly fast and varies little by age, income, or gender. Older Americans use the web for travel planning as often as younger Americans. This means that the highest potential travelers (those older, retired consumers with the greatest disposable income) can be effectively reached via the Internet. According to one study by Stanford University, Internet users spend nearly 10 percent of their online time researching travel sites.

So, how excited were you when your community's website went live? And now that your town has a website, have you wondered about its purpose? If you have a website just because other communities have one, too, that's not good enough. Many towns say that the website is simply an information source for local residents, businesses, and community leaders. But the real power of the Internet lies in its power to promote.

It's rare to find a community that isn't looking for some form of economic growth: residential, business, industry, or tourism. The Internet is the most powerful and cost effective way to market your community.

There are two major challenges with a website: Is it good enough to close the sale? And can your customer even find it?

So how can your area compete on the super highway? Assuming that your community already has something of interest for visitors, there are hundreds of ways to make your site stand out. Here are a few:

- Make the site informational but not wordy. Research has shown that users are more likely to read web content that is concise and factual. Use bullet points.

Victoria, British Columbia's tourism website (this page and opposite) (www.tourismvictoria.com) has an outstanding home page. It's easy to navigate, is clean and elegant, has a central focus, uses world-class photography promoting a range of experiences – all of which pull visitors into the site.

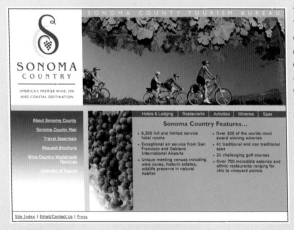

The Sonoma County Tourism Bureau's website (www.sonoma-county.com) does an excellent job of promoting activities using excellent photography, uses quick facts, and is easy to navigate.

- The site should answer any questions that the visitor may have. They want to know, "What is there to do? What does the town look like? How do I get around? Where do I stay? Are there any package deals? Are there special activities for kids, seniors? What's going on this month?"

- Think about organizing your site by activity type from a menu that asks, "What do you want to do?"

- Include testimonials from satisfied visitors —those third-party endorsements we talked about earlier.

- Make your activities guide and other literature available for download as PDF files.

- To ensure large numbers of people visit your site, establish reciprocal links with other tourism-oriented websites and register with the most popular search engines.

- Find a qualified, professional web designer. Go for experience rather than just local. With the Internet, access to every web designer is at the tip of your fingers.

- A good website is meant to showcase your best qualities – the things that make you worth a special trip. Be sure to budget properly. $15,000 to $20,000 is not too much to spend.

- Use lots of photography, especially activity shots. Potential tourists want to get as close to visiting your community as they can without actually setting foot on your sidewalks. Photos will draw people in.

- Purchase key words, often referred to as "pay per click" programs. Eighty percent of Web surfers never go past the first two pages of search results. Pay-per-click can help you be on the first page.

- Promote experiences, not geography. People are looking for activities and seldom for cities. If your town is the bird watching capital of North Carolina, will they find it if they Google "bird watching North Carolina?"

- Market experiences by type of travel (RV, motorcycle, bicycling, private auto, tour bus), by activity (history, culinary, gardening, entertainment, culture, events, etc.), and by season.

- Develop itineraries by type of travel and activity. Do half-day, full-day, two- and three-day itineraries. Include specifics, not generalities.

- Photos should be optimized for quicker downloading. If you want to display a lot of photos on one page, use thumbnail images that users can click if they want to see a larger size.

- Develop an e-newsletter that includes upcoming events and special travel savings. Make it easy to subscribe and unsubscribe. This is "permission marketing" not spam and creates top of mind awareness.

- If your town has the budget, dedicate a person full-time to the web. It's that important. Keep your site fresh, up to date, and ever changing so it doesn't become a "been there, done that" site.

- Travelers use their computers to book flights and reserve rooms. If your site doesn't offer that e-commerce connection, make sure it provides links to sites that do.

The Internet has become a remarkable tool for people who want to plan their vacations from the comfort of their own homes. Nimble fingers and a ready mouse are all it takes. The Internet has also become a marketing tool for communities to encourage people to get out of their homes and see what is great about this country. The Internet may be a great place to let your fingers do the walking, but a great site will convince visitors to let their feet do the walking through your community.

Rule 25

REPETITION GETS RESULTS, REPETITION GETS RESULTS

The rule of frequency

We all have sayings that we live by: "Don't forget to wear clean underwear," or "Don't talk with your mouth full." Our mothers put them in our heads, and even though we ignored them when we were young, we remember them now and pass them on to our children. We remember them not because they were so wise, but because our mothers kept repeating them to us over and over and over again until they sunk in.

In tourism, repetition is often the key to getting people to visit your community. How many times have you heard the announcer approach the most valuable player after the Super Bowl and ask, "Where are you going after the game?" The player then responds, "I'm going to Disneyland!" People have been talking about and making fun of that ad for years. Yet it works. People remember it, and at one time in their lives have probably gone to Disneyland.

Frequency creates Top of Mind Awareness (TOMA). When people think, "Gee, it would be good to get away for a few days," you want your community to be the one that comes to mind. If it's on their minds, it's either because they have been there before, or because they have heard about it enough times for it to register. In the newspaper industry, they sell TOMA packages for this very purpose. When people make decisions to go to a new place, it is more than likely that they have seen or heard about it numerous times.

Ads typically need to be seen five times before they are remembered. You are far better off running an ad in a single magazine five times (or more) than you are running the same ad once in five different publications. At least the readers of the single magazine will remember you; your ad will barely register a blip on the radar of readers with only one exposure.

In order to be successful, your ads and exposure must be frequent. Some of the most effective ads on television would be considered terrible by most standards, but because they are played so often, you remember them. And in tourism, that is the name of the game: be remembered.

Tied to frequency is consistency. While you may see the same photo, the same slogan, the same ad promoting your community time and time again, the customer doesn't see it as often as you do. If there is too much variation between messages, it's the same as running a different ad for a different community each time. And there goes the five times rule. Rather than remembering five distinct messages, each seen only once, the customer will remember none of them. Depending on the campaign, you can easily use the same slogan or concept for two or three years.

Chances are, when people see or hear your ad, they may not be planning a trip or even a quick getaway. But when they do sit down and think about where they would like to go, you want their mind to travel to your town. Say it once, say it twice, then say it again and again. Frequency sells. Repetition gets results. Repetition gets results.

Repetition will create top of mind awareness. You are hoping that your name will become synonymous with your primary lure. When you see the following communities, what's the first thing that comes to mind?

Let's try it the other way around. Here's what some communities are known for. Can you name the community?

- *Nashville, Tennessee*
- *Las Vegas, Nevada*
- *Branson, Missouri*
- *Salem, Massachusetts*
- *Green Bay, Wisconsin*
- *Orlando, Florida*
- *Hershey, Pennsylvania*
- *Hollywood, California*

- *Amish, Dutch*
- *Wine Capital of the U.S.*
- *Federal Government*
- *LDS (Mormon) Church*
- *Tossing salmon at the market*

Want some answers? From top left:
Country Music • Adult Fun • Music theater • Witch trials • the Packers • Disneyworld • Chocolate • Movies
Lancaster, PA • Napa Valley • Washington, DC • Salt Lake City • Seattle's Pike Place Market

Questions for Success:

☐ Is your town using TOMA in its marketing efforts?
☐ When you think of a fast-food restaurant, what's the first name that pops into your mind? Why?
☐ When someone wants to experience what your town has to offer is your community the first place that comes to mind?

The Authors

Roger Brooks is the President of Destination Development, Inc., which specializes in community branding, tourism development, and marketing with offices in Washington and Florida. Over the past 25 years, Roger has assisted more than 400 communities, dozens of counties and states/provinces, and privately developed destination resorts in their efforts to further develop their client base and the tourism industry. Additionally, he has recruited more than $3 billion of private investment to destination resorts and communities, and has amassed an outstanding record of success. His tell-it-like-it-is, bottom-line approach, and tremendous enthusiasm for the industry has empowered organizations around the world in their tourism efforts, and has made Roger one of the most sought after tourism experts in North America.

Maury Forman, Ph.D., is the Director of Education and Training for the Washington State Department of Community, Trade and Economic Development. He was the winner of the American Economic Development Council's Preston Award in 1998 for outstanding contributions in educational advancement, the U.S. Small Business Administration's 1998 Vision 2000 Award, and the ROI Research Institute Award for Innovation in Adult Education. He is a popular speaker across the country and is known as an educator and humorist. Dr. Forman is the author and editor of numerous books on economic development, including Race to Recruit, Learning to Lead, Washington Entrepreneurs Guide, Community Wisdom, How to Create Jobs Now and Beyond 2000, and Journey to Jobs.

The Organizations

Destination Development, Inc.

STATE OF WASHINGTON
DEPARTMENT OF COMMUNITY,
TRADE AND ECONOMIC DEVELOPMENT

Destination Development, Inc. (DDI) is the leading tourism and downtown-development consulting firm in North America. Assisting both public-sector entities and privately developed projects, the award-winning DDI team has become a one-stop-shop for virtually all tourism, community branding, downtown development, and marketing projects. Services include the creation of community branding, development and marketing action plans, performing community and marketing assessments, the creation of branding systems, educational forums, providing downtown redevelopment and repositioning programs, theme development, wayfinding and signage programs, cultural arts and facilities planning, and a host of other tourism and resort-related services.

The Washington State Department of Community, Trade and Economic Development (CTED), is charged with enhancing and promoting sustainable economic vitality throughout Washington State. From services and manufacturing to tourism, CTED invests in Washington's communities, businesses and families to build a healthy and prosperous future.